Table of Contents

Record of Scores—Book C (Unit 18) 3

Summative Test

Phonemic Awareness and Phonics 4

Vocabulary and Morphology 6

Grammar and Usage 10

Progress Indicators

Test of Silent Word Reading Fluency (Form B) 15

DRP® (Degrees of Reading Power) Reading Test (Form C/D-1) 19

Spelling Inventory 26

SOPRIS WEST™ EDUCATIONAL SERVICES
A CAMBIUM LEARNING COMPANY

BOSTON, MA • LONGMONT, CO

Copyright 2005 (Third Edition) by Jane Fell Greene. All rights reserved.

09 08 07 06   10 9 8 7 6 5 4 3

Copyright 2004 by Touchstone Applied Science Associates (TASA), Inc. The DRP® test materials may be used only under the conditions described in the inside cover of the *Assessment Teacher Edition* booklet.

Copyright 2004 by PRO-ED, Inc. The Test of Silent Word Reading Fluency (TOSWRF) materials may be used only under the conditions described in the inside cover of the *Assessment Teacher Edition* booklet.

Copyright 2004 by Pearson Education, Inc. The Spelling Inventory materials may be used only under the conditions described in the inside cover of the *Assessment Teacher Edition* booklet.

No portion of this work may be reproduced or transmitted by any means, electronic or mechanical, including photocopying or recording, or by any information storage and retrieval system, without the express written permission of the publisher.

ISBN 1-57035-542-8

Printed in the United States of America

Published and distributed by

SOPRIS WEST
EDUCATIONAL SERVICES

4093 Specialty Place • Longmont, CO 80504 • (303) 651-2829
www.sopriswest.com

Record of Scores—Book C (Unit 18)

Student's Name: _____

Summative Test—Book C

	Phonemic Awareness and Phonics	Vocabulary and Morphology			Grammar and Usage	
	Word Study	Section 1 Vocabulary	Section 2 Word Relationships	Section 3 Morphology	Section 1 Grammar	Section 2 Sentence Structure
Number Correct / Total # of items	10	5	10	5	10	15
Percent Correct						

Progress Indicators—Book C

	Test of Silent Word Reading Fluency Form B	DRP® Reading Test Form C/D-1	Spelling Inventory
Raw Score	_____	_____	_____
DRP® Unit Score		_____	
Grade Equivalent	_____	_____	

Interpretation and Recommendations

_____
_____
_____
_____

Summative Test

**Phonemic Awareness and Phonics
Section 1—Word Study Part A**

> Look at and listen to each word. Decide whether the underlined syllable is a closed, open, final silent **e**, or **r**-controlled syllable. Fill in the bubble for your answer.
>
> **Sample:** *Listen:* **in ter <u>vene</u>**.
> - Ⓐ closed
> - Ⓑ open
> - Ⓒ final silent **e**
> - Ⓓ **r**-controlled

1. *Listen:* **im <u>ply</u>**.
   - Ⓐ closed
   - Ⓑ open
   - Ⓒ final silent **e**
   - Ⓓ **r**-controlled

2. *Listen:* **can <u>did</u>**.
   - Ⓐ closed
   - Ⓑ open
   - Ⓒ final silent **e**
   - Ⓓ **r**-controlled

3. *Listen:* **<u>or</u> bit**.
   - Ⓐ closed
   - Ⓑ open
   - Ⓒ final silent **e**
   - Ⓓ **r**-controlled

4. *Listen:* **lo <u>cate</u>**.
   - Ⓐ closed
   - Ⓑ open
   - Ⓒ final silent **e**
   - Ⓓ **r**-controlled

5. *Listen:* **<u>e</u> rode**.
   - Ⓐ closed
   - Ⓑ open
   - Ⓒ final silent **e**
   - Ⓓ **r**-controlled

Summative Test

Phonemic Awareness and Phonics
Section 1—Word Study Part B

> Read each syllable. Fill in the bubble for the same syllable type.
>
> **Sample: pro**.
> Ⓐ in
> Ⓑ por
> Ⓒ pre
> Ⓓ cape

6. **ert**
   Ⓐ cur
   Ⓑ tom
   Ⓒ riv
   Ⓓ take

7. **con**
   Ⓐ id
   Ⓑ hu
   Ⓒ vite
   Ⓓ ern

8. **lete**
   Ⓐ po
   Ⓑ mote
   Ⓒ ter
   Ⓓ min

9. **be**
   Ⓐ pose
   Ⓑ jack
   Ⓒ pi
   Ⓓ sir

10. **chan**
    Ⓐ mar
    Ⓑ ra
    Ⓒ clued
    Ⓓ ex

Summative Test

Vocabulary and Morphology
Section 1—Vocabulary

> Look at and listen to each sentence. Select the correct meaning for the underlined word in each sentence and fill in the bubble for your answer.
>
> **Sample:** *Listen:* The <u>bat</u> is made of wood.
>   Ⓐ an animal
>   Ⓑ an action
>   Ⓒ a piece of sports equipment

11. *Listen:* Art will <u>cart</u> dirt into the garden.
    Ⓐ an action
    Ⓑ a vehicle
    Ⓒ a body part

12. *Listen:* Herbert can name the <u>states</u>.
    Ⓐ parts of our country
    Ⓑ an action
    Ⓒ a toy

13. *Listen:* Rosa was <u>second</u> in line.
    Ⓐ a part of a minute
    Ⓑ the position after first
    Ⓒ to agree

14. *Listen:* Flora brought Alice a <u>favor</u> from the party.
    Ⓐ to show support
    Ⓑ a kind act
    Ⓒ a small gift

15. *Listen:* The teacher made a <u>copy</u> of the page in the math book.
    Ⓐ to imitate
    Ⓑ a reproduction
    Ⓒ a radio code

Summative Test

Vocabulary and Morphology
Section 2—Word Relationships Part A

> Look at the pairs of words. Decide which of the answers describes the relationship between the two words. Fill in the bubble for your answer.
>
> **Sample: happiness: sadness**
> - Ⓐ synonyms
> - Ⓑ antonyms
> - Ⓒ neither

16. **remember: forget**
    - Ⓐ synonyms
    - Ⓑ antonyms
    - Ⓒ neither

17. **minute: moment**
    - Ⓐ synonyms
    - Ⓑ antonyms
    - Ⓒ neither

18. **primitive: modern**
    - Ⓐ synonyms
    - Ⓑ antonyms
    - Ⓒ neither

19. **protect: defend**
    - Ⓐ synonyms
    - Ⓑ antonyms
    - Ⓒ neither

20. **demote: deliver**
    - Ⓐ synonyms
    - Ⓑ antonyms
    - Ⓒ neither

Summative Test

Vocabulary and Morphology
Section 2—Word Relationships Part B

> Look at the pairs of words. Decide which of the answers has the same meaning as the word pairs. Fill in the bubble for your answer.
>
> **Sample: bunny, rabbit**
> - Ⓐ squirrel
> - Ⓑ hare
> - Ⓒ illness

21. **livid, angry**
    - Ⓐ lazy
    - Ⓑ upset
    - Ⓒ brave

22. **still, quiet**
    - Ⓐ silent
    - Ⓑ restless
    - Ⓒ active

23. **make, construct**
    - Ⓐ conduct
    - Ⓑ connect
    - Ⓒ form

24. **permit, consent**
    - Ⓐ project
    - Ⓑ decline
    - Ⓒ let

25. **help, assist**
    - Ⓐ support
    - Ⓑ harm
    - Ⓒ react

Summative Test

Vocabulary and Morphology
Section 3—Morphology

> Read each sentence to yourself. Decide which prefix makes sense in the sentence and fill in the bubble for your answer.
>
> **Sample:** The plane will ___part from Gate 26 at ten.
> - Ⓐ de
> - Ⓑ ex
> - Ⓒ re
> - Ⓓ non

26. The babysitter ___vised the children.
    - Ⓐ re
    - Ⓑ super
    - Ⓒ con
    - Ⓓ un

27. We ___port food to China.
    - Ⓐ ex
    - Ⓑ re
    - Ⓒ de
    - Ⓓ over

28. Miss Pitt demanded a ___ply to her question.
    - Ⓐ non
    - Ⓑ in
    - Ⓒ re
    - Ⓓ ex

29. The trip was ___stop from Toronto to Boston.
    - Ⓐ un
    - Ⓑ de
    - Ⓒ re
    - Ⓓ non

30. Al and Stan will ___act during the play.
    - Ⓐ inter
    - Ⓑ de
    - Ⓒ non
    - Ⓓ super

Summative Test

Grammar and Usage
Section 1—Grammar Part A

> Look at and listen to the sentences and decide if the underlined word is an adjective, adverb, preposition, or none of these. Fill in the bubble for your answer.
>
> **Sample:** *Listen:* The cloud floated <u>over</u> the fields.
> - Ⓐ adjective
> - Ⓑ adverb
> - Ⓒ preposition
> - Ⓓ none of the above

31. *Listen:* The <u>frisky</u> pup jumped through the snowdrift.
    - Ⓐ adjective
    - Ⓑ adverb
    - Ⓒ preposition
    - Ⓓ none of the above

32. *Listen:* The mascot was <u>lively</u>.
    - Ⓐ adjective
    - Ⓑ adverb
    - Ⓒ preposition
    - Ⓓ none of the above

33. *Listen:* <u>During</u> the storm, the wind howled.
    - Ⓐ adjective
    - Ⓑ adverb
    - Ⓒ preposition
    - Ⓓ none of the above

34. *Listen:* Tom <u>chose</u> the calico cat.
    - Ⓐ adjective
    - Ⓑ adverb
    - Ⓒ preposition
    - Ⓓ none of the above

35. *Listen:* The box <u>with</u> a bow is a gift.
    - Ⓐ adjective
    - Ⓑ adverb
    - Ⓒ preposition
    - Ⓓ none of the above

Summative Test

Grammar and Usage
Section 1—Grammar Part B

> Read each sentence. Decide of the underlined word is a main verb, helping verb, or neither. Fill in the bubble for your answer.
>
> **Sample:** I <u>am</u> selling tickets.
> - Ⓐ main verb
> - Ⓑ helping verb
> - Ⓒ neither

36. The plant <u>had</u> a dozen blossoms.
    - Ⓐ main verb
    - Ⓑ helping verb
    - Ⓒ neither

37. The program <u>was</u> going to be a success.
    - Ⓐ main verb
    - Ⓑ helping verb
    - Ⓒ neither

38. They <u>explored</u> the continent.
    - Ⓐ main verb
    - Ⓑ helping verb
    - Ⓒ neither

39. We <u>did</u> make a plan for our project.
    - Ⓐ main verb
    - Ⓑ helping verb
    - Ⓒ neither

40. I <u>am</u> ten minutes late for school.
    - Ⓐ main verb
    - Ⓑ helping verb
    - Ⓒ neither

Summative Test

Grammar and Usage
Section 2—Sentence Structure Part A

> **Sample:** Read the two sentences. Underline the **direct object** in each sentence. Write a **compound direct object** sentence using one of the conjunctions: **and**, **but**, **or**. Underline the conjunction used in the sentence.
>
> He won a record album. He won a ticket to the rodeo.
>
> _____

41. Read the two sentences. Write a **compound sentence** using one of these conjunctions: **and**, **but**, **or**. Underline the conjunction used in the sentence.

    I like sunny summer days. I don't like dark winter days.

    _____

42. Read the two sentences. Underline the **predicate** in each sentence. Write a **compound predicate sentence** using one of these conjunctions: **and, but, or**. Underline the conjunction used in the sentence.

    Tony will correct his paper. Tony will record his score.

    _____

43. Read the two sentences. Underline the **indirect objects**. Write a **compound indirect object sentence** using one of these conjunctions: **and, but, or**. Underline the conjunction used in the sentence.

    Her parents could give him the kitten. Her parents could give her the kitten.

    _____

44. Read the two sentences. Underline the **subject** in each sentence. Write a **compound subject sentence** using one of these conjunctions: **and, but, or**. Underline the conjunction used in the sentence.

    Computers are used in the classrooms. Books are used in the classrooms.

    _____

45. Read the two sentences. Underline the **direct object** in each sentence. Write a **compound direct object sentence** using one of these conjunctions: **and, but, or**. Underline the conjunction used in the sentence.

    Sybil could order a ham salad sandwich. Sybil could order a hamburger.

    _____

Summative Test

Grammar and Usage
Section 2—Sentence Structure Part B

> Read the sentences to yourself. Choose the verb that best completes the sentence and fill in the bubble for your answer.
>
> **Sample:** The milk _____ spilled on the table.
> - Ⓐ are
> - Ⓑ had
> - Ⓒ did
> - Ⓓ have

46. A bad storm _____ harm to the crops on the farm.
    - Ⓐ does
    - Ⓑ have
    - Ⓒ are
    - Ⓓ is

47. The mantis _____ an insect.
    - Ⓐ are
    - Ⓑ do
    - Ⓒ is
    - Ⓓ had

48. The farmer _____ forgotten to close the gate.
    - Ⓐ is
    - Ⓑ had
    - Ⓒ was
    - Ⓓ have

49. Bob and Ana _____ standing on the vast hillside.
    - Ⓐ can
    - Ⓑ was
    - Ⓒ were
    - Ⓓ is

50. Today, she _____ play lacrosse with her classmate.
    - Ⓐ are
    - Ⓑ was
    - Ⓒ can
    - Ⓓ had

Summative Test

Grammar and Usage
Section 2—Sentence Structure Part C

> Look at and listen to the sentences. Decide whether the underlined word is used as a subject, direct object, indirect object, or none of the above. Fill in the bubble for your answer.
>
> **Sample:** *Listen:* Jan gave the <u>dog</u> a bone.
> - Ⓐ subject
> - Ⓑ direct object
> - Ⓒ indirect object
> - Ⓓ none of the above

51. *Listen:* The <u>class</u> saw a prehistoric insect fossil in the quartzite.
    - Ⓐ subject
    - Ⓑ direct object
    - Ⓒ indirect object
    - Ⓓ none of the above

52. *Listen:* The quarterback didn't toss the <u>ball</u> to the fullback.
    - Ⓐ subject
    - Ⓑ direct object
    - Ⓒ indirect object
    - Ⓓ none of the above

53. *Listen:* They watched a <u>yak</u> on their trip.
    - Ⓐ subject
    - Ⓑ direct object
    - Ⓒ indirect object
    - Ⓓ none of the above

54. *Listen:* They have a <u>bulldog</u> for a pet.
    - Ⓐ subject
    - Ⓑ direct object
    - Ⓒ indirect object
    - Ⓓ none of the above

55. *Listen:* Al told his <u>sister</u> a story.
    - Ⓐ subject
    - Ⓑ direct object
    - Ⓒ indirect object
    - Ⓓ none of the above

Summative Test

Test of Silent Word Reading Fluency (Form B)

Record of Scores

	Raw Score	Grade Equivalent
Silent Word Reading Fluency—Form B	_____	_____

Student Responses

Example 1   in yes go me see

Example 2   ofgoliketwobig/
onheupyesget/

Adapted with permission from *Test of Silent Word Reading Fluency*, by N. Mather, D. Hammill, E. Allen, and R. Roberts, 2004, Austin, TX: PRO-ED, Inc. ©2004 by PRO-ED, Inc.

Summative Test

When your teacher says to begin, turn the page and start the test.

Progress Indicators

seeheinmygogetdoupgreentwodress/
newflewletflytaketreebuyguessput/
overwhystaypeoplebagtryduckourall/
auntlunchsuncrycouldfiveprizehurry/
nightbygivecountcentpopkeptreal/
oakbuildemptyfullsentdeepablenut/
restwaghurtquietfoodkeyrivercomb/
freepoundaimnetrichserveagepurple/
dreweaglebullarrivepolestemfault/
yetsceneoilclubgiraffeagreepolar/
urgebuckobjectdullcreepteafrymop/
wigresultlickacreicysnarlhogeffect/
woundglueaffectpoemreflectboulder/
jugnervehuddlekeenvoteoysteryelp/
apefileclutchsnugenvythudmiracle/
dueoozehuewafflejestbazaarrigpelt/
yielddiaryimpgemcyclebaldslimliar/
vestouncelardreapnickarckilntrophy/
siegehubdetectwiltcuethreshsulklilt/
accessgaudyswivelpivotrelicverdict/
edibleprivacyirkerrfestivedulyrove/
staunchcliquephysiquedivulge/
slurcultnaivebaublehysteriaroster/
girthdeficientfeignensemblefoible/
bolsterfettercommuneglutviebier/
negligibleneuteressencelibelquibble/
precludepreceptvernacularjuncture/
tertiarysecularvolublepulsarguile/
duresssullywreakepochdubcoerce/
symposiumrazeimbuequaffgirdacquiesce/
egressfacileneophytecajolefecund/
encomiumpecuniaryimbrogliojocund/

©2004 by PRO-ED, Inc. All rights reserved.

Form B

DRP® Reading Test

Directions to Student

This is a test to find out how well you read. The test contains passages for you to read. Words are missing from the passages. Wherever a word is missing, there is a blank line with a number on it. Next to the passage, you will find the same number and five words. Choose the word that makes the best sense in the blank.

Next to the word, fill in the bubble for the answer you have chosen.

Read Sample **S-1** below and see how the right answer has been marked in your booklet. Then read Sample **S-2** and fill in the bubble next to the correct answer.

Record of Scores			
	Raw Score	DRP® Unit Score	Grade Equivalent
DRP® Reading Test—Form C/D-1	_____	_____	_____

Samples

It was sunny and hot for days. Then the ___S-1___ changed. It turned cloudy and cool.

S-1 Ⓐ price   Ⓑ road   Ⓒ job   ● weather   Ⓔ size

It isn't safe to go out today. There was too much ___S-2___ yesterday. Many streets are flooded with water.

S-2 Ⓐ rain   Ⓑ food   Ⓒ mail   Ⓓ noise   Ⓔ work

Look at the answer for Sample **S-1**. The letter **D** is filled in because the word **weather** makes the best sense in the blank.

For Sample **S-2** you should have filled in the bubble for the letter **A** because the word **rain** makes the best sense in the blank.

As you can see, you may not be sure of the answer until you have read the sentences that come after the blank. So be sure to read enough to choose your answer.

Progress Indicators

DRP® Reading Test

You are not expected to read at the same speed as other students or to answer the same number of items. As you work on this test, you will find that the passages become harder to read. Do your best to read as many passages as you can and to answer as many items as you can. Work carefully and do not rush. You will be given as much time as you need.

Remember, mark only one answer for each item. If you want to change an answer, be sure to erase or cross out your first mark. Then mark the answer you want.

The oldest surviving sea charts date to about 1300 A.D. It is believed that there probably were earlier charts. However, these have not been found. Some of the missing charts may have been destroyed in storms. Some may have been __1__ in other ways. They may simply have worn out. Others may have been thrown overboard to avoid capture.

The earliest sea charts showed where safe harbors could be found in the Mediterranean. They also warned of hazards. The charts showed underwater rocks that might wreck ships. They showed other __2__, too. They pictured reefs or shoals where ships might run aground.

These charts helped sailors get their bearings. Islands, cliffs, and many places along the shore were shown. Coastal areas were crowded with information. Other __3__ were not. Inland, away from shore, few details were given. Mountain ranges and cities far from the sea were sometimes left out altogether.

Sea charts were not drawn simply in black and white. Instead, chartmakers __4__ them. Safe harbors were shown in red. Green, blue, yellow, and brown were employed for certain land and water features. Red and green also appeared in the "wind roses." These were flower-shaped emblems drawn on the charts. Lines extended out from the roses, like a sun's rays. These lines were not meant to be decorative. They were meant to be __5__. They aided navigation by showing wind direction. Following the lines with a compass, sailors could stay on course.

Until the 15th century, sea charts were drawn by hand, one at a time. There was no other way to __6__ them. When maps were made this way, it was hard to keep all copies the same. As copies were drawn, details were dropped. Errors appeared. When a chart was copied, changes that had been made before were repeated. New ones were added. The __7__ multiplied. The map grew less accurate as time passed. Eventually, printing presses put an end to this problem.

1 Ⓐ bound Ⓑ marked Ⓒ lost Ⓓ shaped Ⓔ manufactured

2 Ⓐ dangers Ⓑ borders Ⓒ numbers Ⓓ colonies Ⓔ capitals

3 Ⓐ scales Ⓑ regions Ⓒ boats Ⓓ captains Ⓔ travelers

4 Ⓐ checked Ⓑ folded Ⓒ framed Ⓓ titled Ⓔ colored

5 Ⓐ short Ⓑ narrow Ⓒ flat Ⓓ useful Ⓔ faint

6 Ⓐ roll Ⓑ read Ⓒ clean Ⓓ produce Ⓔ preserve

7 Ⓐ costs Ⓑ mistakes Ⓒ vessels Ⓓ libraries Ⓔ populations

(Go to the Next Page)

The schooling of fish is at once a very common and a very remarkable sight. Hundreds of fish will glide by in unison. They seem to move more like a single organism than a group of individuals. Suddenly the whole school veers to the side, all at the same instant. Not a single fish is __8__. Moreover, as they go, they maintain a constant distance from one another.

8 Ⓐ born Ⓑ affected Ⓒ left Ⓓ located Ⓔ recognized

Scientists have been studying the schooling of fish to find out more about this phenomenon. For one thing, they want to know the reason that fish form schools. Is there some benefit to swimming in groups? If so, what is the __9__?

9 Ⓐ current Ⓑ advantage Ⓒ limit Ⓓ sign Ⓔ taste

Scientists think schooling is helpful to smaller fish because it allows them to get away from predators. Confronting a large group seems to confuse a predator. When a predator faces a large number of swiftly moving prey, it has trouble choosing a victim. It cannot __10__ quickly. While the predator tries to select a prey, the smaller fish have an extra second to get away. This enables them to __11__.

10 Ⓐ decide Ⓑ rise Ⓒ breathe Ⓓ turn Ⓔ wake

11 Ⓐ feed Ⓑ float Ⓒ escape Ⓓ hunt Ⓔ finish

How, though, do the fish manage to stay the same distance apart? One scientist put dark lenses over the eyes of several fish to blind them temporarily. Thus, the fish could not __12__. Yet they could still swim in the school.

12 Ⓐ eat Ⓑ pass Ⓒ see Ⓓ live Ⓔ leap

The __13__ was valuable. It showed that vision is not a fish's only cue to position. Fish have a sense organ that people do not have. This organ is called the lateral-line canal. It responds to changes in water pressure, permitting a fish to judge the speed and distance of its neighbors. The canal provides the fish with __14__. These sensory data help a fish to keep its place within the school.

13 Ⓐ oil Ⓑ skin Ⓒ vessel Ⓓ increase Ⓔ experiment

14 Ⓐ food Ⓑ pleasure Ⓒ shelter Ⓓ nothing Ⓔ information

(Go to the Next Page)

Infectious disease occurs in plants when a living organism, called the pathogen, invades the plant and impairs its function by feeding on it. For this to occur, a host plant and pathogen must, by definition, be present. They are not sufficient, however. Something else is __15__. To ensure that the pathogen enters the host, a proper environment is also essential, as the following case illustrates.

15 Ⓐ required Ⓑ created Ⓒ described Ⓓ shared Ⓔ discovered

Until the 1700s, the European larch tree was uncultivated. It grew wild in the higher mountains of central Europe. Then larch began being planted extensively. Ship builders prized this durable wood, which was resistant to sea water. Other wood decayed before vessels were many years old, but that wasn't true of larch. Instead, larch __16__. After 50 years, it remained usable.

16 Ⓐ smelled Ⓑ lasted Ⓒ burned Ⓓ yellowed Ⓔ flowered

In the 19th century, scars appeared on cultivated larches, deforming the wood. Nobody knew why the scars appeared until botanists investigated. They soon found the __17__. Reproductive cells of a fungus were being blown onto the larches. The fungus sprouted tiny tendrils into any available injury. It could not enter unblemished trees. There had to be a __18__. Inside, the tendrils spread to feed on nutrients under the bark. Scars marked the location of the fungus.

17 Ⓐ place Ⓑ fruit Ⓒ forest Ⓓ cause Ⓔ total

18 Ⓐ fire Ⓑ stream Ⓒ wound Ⓓ delay Ⓔ crop

The fungus invaded wild mountain larches, too. However, wild trees were affected much less frequently than cultivated ones. In fact, they were rarely __19__. Why should this have been so?

19 Ⓐ dusted Ⓑ removed Ⓒ fenced Ⓓ examined Ⓔ attacked

Environmental conditions were the reason. Wild larches grew at high elevations, where spring was cool, whereas cultivated larches grew lower down, where spring was warmer. This __20__ was critical. In the chill mountain air, trees budded late and leaves toughened quickly. Lower down, warmer weather brought early budding and slow leafing. Leaves at the lower elevations did toughen eventually. However, it took more __21__. For weeks the shoots remained tender. Insects and late frosts damaged the foliage. The fungus entered the weakened leaves and then spread to injuries in the branches and trunk.

20 Ⓐ seed Ⓑ age Ⓒ care Ⓓ shape Ⓔ difference

21 Ⓐ time Ⓑ soil Ⓒ room Ⓓ strength Ⓔ attention

(Go to the Next Page)

By lore and by experience, mineral prospectors in the western United States knew that certain kinds of terrain deserved their attention. Regions that were arid by nature, especially the rugged sectors of such country, were likely to contain mineral deposits. Other __22__ were not. Searching such terrain, prospectors would look for signs of mineralization. They knew that different salts painted rocks in characteristic hues: brown or yellow for iron, green or blue for copper, black for manganese, and lilac for cobalt. The rusty brown of hematite was considered a signpost for gold. Hence, __23__ was important. It indicated where valuable minerals might lie.

If no promising ledges appeared, attention turned to streams and gullies. These might contain "float," gold particles washed down from lodes by streams and rivers. Gold was most frequently found where streams turned, widened, or otherwise lost speed. Where currents slowed, the water could no longer carry gold along. Therefore, the gold __24__. Sinking to the bottom, it gradually became embedded. Sometimes the gold was found as large nuggets, sometimes as fine dust. Such differences in __25__ were meaningful. They indicated how far the gold had traveled. The farther it had gone, the smaller the pieces.

When "float" was found, miners would place some of the gold-bearing dirt in a pan of water and swirl the pan. Sand and other siliceous material washed over the side, leaving only gold and other heavy minerals behind. Gold particles could then be separated from the rest. This was the most common way of __26__ gold. It was called "panning."

Not all gold-bearing river or stream beds had water flowing in them. Some were __27__. Geological changes over the centuries had diverted the water, exposing the beds. While this made digging easier, water needed for panning was often scarce. It was therefore agreed that nobody would be allowed to monopolize the supply. Rather, water would be __28__. Miners would divide the available supply among themselves.

22 (A) animals (B) metals (C) areas (D) costs (E) workers

23 (A) time (B) distance (C) color (D) shape (E) price

24 (A) melted (B) glowed (C) weathered (D) formed (E) settled

25 (A) position (B) soil (C) machinery (D) size (E) temperature

26 (A) obtaining (B) selling (C) protecting (D) shipping (E) weighing

27 (A) dry (B) narrow (C) flat (D) deep (E) dangerous

28 (A) removed (B) boiled (C) wasted (D) shared (E) bottled

©2004 by Touchstone Applied Science (TASA) Inc. This test may be used only under conditions described in the inside cover of *Assessment: Teacher Edition*.

GPR–81–1
Form CD–1

(Go to the Next Page)

In the early 1920s the German mark, once among the world's stablest currencies, became virtually worthless. It deteriorated largely as a result of staggering reparation payments and trade penalties imposed by the Versailles Treaty. Payment of reparations for war damages was not unusual in and of itself. However, the __29__ in this case was extraordinary. The Allied Reparation Commission demanded nearly $35 billion, which many considered far beyond Germany's ability to pay.

29 Ⓐ leader Ⓑ victory Ⓒ crowd Ⓓ amount Ⓔ discovery

The treaty badly hurt Germany's commercial capability. Facing deficits, postwar governments followed the practice, begun during the war, of issuing paper currency to meet expenses. Accordingly, large sums of money were __30__. With paper marks pouring from the presses, Germany experienced an unparalleled inflation. Before the war, the mark was worth about 25 cents. However, this __31__ was not maintained. By 1921, the mark was worth only a penny and by 1922, one hundredth of a cent.

30 Ⓐ buried Ⓑ printed Ⓒ seized Ⓓ shared Ⓔ claimed

31 Ⓐ army Ⓑ value Ⓒ hate Ⓓ service Ⓔ production

As prices soared, laborers dragged their wages in sacks to the grocery, only to find that even the cheapest goods were priced beyond their means. It was nearly impossible to __32__ anything. Everything was too expensive. Pensioners, workers, and the middle class were hard hit by the inflation. Yet not everyone __33__. Speculators, purchasing on credit and repaying in inflated currency, profited greatly.

32 Ⓐ buy Ⓑ hide Ⓒ preserve Ⓓ grow Ⓔ manufacture

33 Ⓐ waited Ⓑ refused Ⓒ helped Ⓓ returned Ⓔ suffered

The situation worsened when France, citing a technical default in reparations, occupied the Ruhr and imposed an economic blockade, not only depriving Germany of that economically vital valley, but also cutting off the Rhineland. The loss of these __34__ was devastating. Without the resources and output of these areas, Germany's economy was crippled.

34 Ⓐ regions Ⓑ bridges Ⓒ troops Ⓓ strikes Ⓔ liberties

By November 1923, the mark fell to 4.2 trillion to the dollar. People took to barter, and food riots and political demonstrations erupted. The Allies became alarmed, fearing an extremist takeover unless they intervened to improve conditions. The Allies therefore __35__ Germany. Loans were made to industry and the reparations schedule eased, allowing Germany to issue a sound new currency.

35 Ⓐ aided Ⓑ mapped Ⓒ fined Ⓓ skirted Ⓔ searched

(Stop)

Progress Indicators

Spelling Inventory

Record of Scores	
	Raw Score
Spelling Inventory	_____

Student Responses

Write the words that your teacher dictates.

1. _____
2. _____
3. _____
4. _____
5. _____
6. _____
7. _____
8. _____
9. _____
10. _____
11. _____
12. _____
13. _____
14. _____
15. _____
16. _____
17. _____
18. _____
19. _____
20. _____
21. _____
22. _____
23. _____
24. _____
25. _____
26. _____
27. _____
28. _____
29. _____
30. _____